Building the Nation
and other poems

Christopher Henry Muwanga Barlow

Fountain Publishers

Fountain Publishers Ltd
P.O. Box 488
Kampala

© C.H.M. Barlow 2000
First published 2000

All rights reserved. No part of this publication may be reproduced, stored in a retrieval system, or transmitted in any form or by any means, electronic, mechanical, photocopying, recording or otherwise, without prior written permission of the publishers.

ISBN   9970 02 191 5

Dedication

In memory of John Barlow, my father;
Jack and Jane, my siblings;
Fay and Chris, my offspring.

Contents

PART I: POLITICIANS, SERVANTS AND SYCOPHANTS

Acknowledgement	iv
Foreword	vi

My newest bride	1
Foreign aid	4
Building the nation	7
The leader that hung	9
Evenings on safari	11
The bullock	13
Of feathers and dead leaves	13
Craving for dawn	14
The ride to Chichicastenango	15
Chichicastenango revisited	17
The interrupted dream	18
Cameleon, leopard and blue-headed lizard	20
Of fawning dogs and the purring cats	21
Paper napkin	22
Bear the fools and the stupid kindly	23
Uganda	24
Fifty four	26
Summit fever I: Father to son	27
Summit fever II: Brother to brother	32
Summit fever III: Epilogue	36
It continues to rain and the grass is green	37
Jubilating South African democracy	38

PART II: THE JUNGLES OF HUMANITY

Vietnam	39
The jungles of Biafra	41
The flight	45

PART III: ARGUMENTS WITH GOD

The image of God	47
God is magic	47
Argument with God	48
An honest prayer to God	50
Crucifixion	52
Palm Sunday 1985	54
Tussling with truth	55

PART IV: RANDOM PORTRAITS

Portrait of a young girl	58
Nnassuuna the country girl	59
The singer	60
Errand to Sibemalizibwa	62
My boss	63
White lizards	64
New York	65
Old Mousey	66
Hanlon	68
Meeting my soul-brother	70
Fay	72
My grandmother's eyes	72
Growing into a lizard	73

PART V: OF NATURE

Masaaba from Nkokonjeru	74
Rainy morning	75
The death of an eland	76
Naked Meru	77
Laughter at death	78
Desirable war	79
Rain at daybreak	80

PART VI: THE RICH LIVE AMALGAM

When I am dead and gone	82
Uganda from Oxford	83
The village well	85
Eating alone	87
The bull	88
The horse	89
Tears for Taurus	91
Magic	96
The things I miss	97
The insolent slave	99
Fits of depression	100
I refuse to take your brotherly hand	101
Mosquito and I	103
Women - my bane	106
The tenth commandment	107
Not forever courageously	108
The simmering amalgam	109

PART VII: OF LOVE AND ALL THAT

Our love	111
The reunion	112
To the persistent ghost	113
Assault	114
Love for Margaret	115
Moments that live forever	116
I dare not pull you apart	117

Acknowledgement

I wish to express my very sincere gratitude to some people. First and foremost, my thanks go to the late Dennis G.R. Herbert (who later became Lord Hemingford). Lord Hemingford was a very good teacher. He enjoyed teaching so much that although he was then the headmaster of King's College Budo, he allocated himself actual teaching schedules on top of his heavy administrative duties. His lively teaching of poetry was responsible for stimulating my enjoyment, and later writing of poetry.

My interest in poetry was further developed by my professors and lecturers at Makerere, notably Professor and Mrs Alan Warner and Mrs M. Macpherson.

I have to thank the distinguished poet, the late Prof. Okot p'Bitek, my friends the late Pio and his wife Erivaniya Zirimu, Prof. David Rubadiri and Prof. David Cook for organising the literature festivals and conferences and persuading me, in the sixties, to expose my poems in those meetings.

Special thanks go to my friend Ibbo Mandaza, Director General of SAPES TRUST (1989), for publishing fourteen of my poems under the title *Of Feathers and Dead Leaves*. I read most of the poems in the small collection as my contribution to the reminiscences of what African administrations had gone through in the twenty-five years since the inception of the African Association for Public Administration and Management (AAPAM) in 1962. As a result of the response, Ibbo Mandaza offered to publish the poems.

Sincere thanks also go to Susan Kiguli, lecturer in the Department of Literature, Makerere University, and fellow poet for reading through this collection and for her comments. She also organised an extremely well attended reading session of a select number of my poems on November 20, 1998, which received a most enthusiastic response, which further encouraged me to publish.

I am deeply grateful to Irene Nambafu who put all these poems on computer in her spare time whilst doing her demanding work.

I wish to acknowledge and express my gratitude to the members of my family for their encouragement and assistance in the final preparation of the manuscript.

Sincere thanks go to my wife, Fayce, for useful suggestions which added clarity to my work. Also to my brother Hugo, who with his deep mind, suggested improvements to a number of poems. His persistence in encouraging me to publish finally wore down my shyness to expose these poems, some of which are very personal.

My daughter Maliza incorporated the numerous final amendments and my daughter Estella designed the book cover. To both of them I say 'Thank you'.

C.H.M.B.

Foreword

These poems, written over a span of over forty-five years, were written for myself. I had no intention of publishing them when they were being written or after they had been written. Over time, however, I have been persuaded to publish a few of them and now almost all of them.

I enjoyed writing some of them. With others I agonised and had to dig deep into my inner self in an effort to understand myself, the people, situations, the paradoxes and dilemmas, the re-occuring question for which I had no easy or obvious explanations. I agonised in the search for the simple words that could aptly express the intensity and vividness of the irrepressible feelings that kept simmering in my mind, sometimes for years!

C.H.M. Barlow
Kampala

The following poems have been published elsewhere before

My newest bride, Errand to Sibemalizibwa as *The news* and *Argument with God*. First published in ***In Black and White*** collected by David Cook, Nairobi: East African Literature Bureau, 1976.

The interrupted dream, Building the nation. Published in ZUKA - A journal of East African Creative Writings, Nairobi: Oxford University Press, October 1970.

Building the nation, The death of an eland, I refused to take your brotherly hand, The village well. Published in ***Poems from East Africa***, Edited by David Cook and David Rubadiri Heinemann Educational Books: London (1971).

Building the nation published in ***An Introduction to East African Poetry*** by Jonathan Kariara and Ellen Kitonga, London: Oxford University Press, 1976.

My newest bride, Foreign aid, Building the nation, From the voter with love, I refused to take your brotherly hand, The bullock, The bull, Tears for Taurus, Offeahers and dead leaves, Craving for dawn, 49, Uganda, Fifty four, It continues to rain and the grass is greener. Published in ***Of feathers and Dead Leaves and other poems***, C.H.M. Barlow, Harare: SAPES TRUST 1989.

Building the nation. Published in ***Growing up with Poetry***, edited by David Rubadiri, Heinemann: Nairobi.

Uganda from Oxford, The flight, Building the nation. Published in ***Uganda Poetry Anthology 2000***, edited by Okot Benge and Alex Bangirana, Fountain: Kampala 2000.

PART I

POLITICIANS, SERVANTS AND SYCOPHANTS

My newest bride

They came in hordes singing her name.
Voices grew hoarse praising her beauty
Her charm was beyond all compare
Her soft touch soothed all pain
Her words taught all wisdom
And her embrace brought eternal bliss.

Moved to fever pitch, I swore,
I swore before the gathered village,
I swore on the bones of my forefathers
That I would neither sleep nor rest
Until she was my wife, my betrothed.

It was a fever, as virulent a fever as you ever saw,
For I ask you my friends, my brothers,
Know you of any fool
Who paid the bride price I paid
Not ever having set eyes on the girl?

And what a bride price!
Facing Greener guns with stones,
Long prison sentences without trial,
Hunger strikes, deportation, the lot!
But I paid, I paid every cent of it.

At last she came, my bride came!
The drums throbbed, they throbbed for a week.
The village sang and drank,
We danced and laughed,
And drank and laughed and danced again.
She was beautiful beyond compare!

Her sparkling eyes,
Her firm warm breasts
Her beautiful smile and merry laughter
Spelt beauty and joy for ever.

When I touched her hand
Currents raced tingling through me.
I kissed her,
All was oblivion but those lips.
Oh! she was so beautiful!

But alas! alas my friends,
Time, that tireless teacher,
Time, the insatiable killer of joy,
And patient healer of all fevers,
Taught me my bride was a woman!

Alas she is a woman,
A woman like my other wives,
Why can't she be a bride for ever?
Why must she be like the others?
Must she join the harem?

We no longer speak of our love
But only of problems and work, work, work!
There is no longer time for thought or rest
She has decreed against any recreation
Her dictatorial demands have usurped all leisure.

Must I toil and sweat without pause,
So our children can read?
Must I raise my voice in anger,
And sharpen my arrows and spears,

So my rich greedy neighbours,
May not snatch her from me?

Must I forfeit my treasured leisure,
Must I spend sleepless nights,
Must my flying hours of youth
Be spent in cold calculating thought,
Must I age before my years,
So our homestead compares with others?

Oh that I could divorce you!
But God forbid! How could I say so!
Oh! Uhuru my love, my sweet,
You are my bane, my life,
I love and hate you,
Your clutch is unrelenting
Uhuru my love, my Freedom.

Foreign aid

Give it its real name
It's not aid for heaven's sake!
Aid indeed!!
   What aid?
   To who?

Call it export promotion
Or supplier's credit;
Add "foreign" in brackets;
For that makes sense.
   But not aid;
   It's not aid.

Yet when the negotiators arrive,
Those dedicated promoters,
It is the red carpet all the way.
Chauffeur driven limousines!
And smart cocktail parties,
Safaris to game parks;
As if it was a necessity
To include the animals,
Birds, fish and the beauty
Of Africa in the negotiations!

In the Conference Room a strip-tease
You must perform for them,
"Strip off your clothes," the economist barks,
"So your economic growth is exposed.
Now perform the Tausa dance
So the debts you may be hiding
Between your buttocks may come to light!"

This, from your former expatriate colleague!
"What is your income?"
"Do you smoke or engage in similar
Frivolities which are beyond your budget?"
"You know you should not, but,
How much do you spend on luxuries?"

"Is Mao your friend?
Is Johnson, or Kosygin?
Is Wilson?
How about De Gaulle?"

You may survive all this
But if you do, that's not all.
Then they proceed to prescribe
(For the sake of their 'aid')
What and what not to eat
And how to conduct your affairs.
"You must eat less social services
So your economic growth is balanced;
But you must have more schools
So 'aid' can be fully assimilated
And have better medical attention
So you can put in a full day's work.

On no account whatsoever
Must you eat any more dates
For debts have to be repaid,
But most important,
Whether suitable or not,
You must buy our goods
For this is the essence of our aid."
When they are finally airborne,

In real strong liquor you must
Drown your pent-up humiliation.
Or else let them out by
Shouting like a lunatic.
That is foreign aid.
      Aid indeed!!

1968

Building the nation

Today I did my share
In building the nation.
I drove a Permanent Secretary
To an important urgent function;
In fact to a luncheon at the Vic.

The menu reflected its importance:
Cold Bell beer with small talk,
Then fried chicken with niceties,
Wine to fill the hollowness of the laughs,
Ice-cream to cover the stereotype jokes,
Coffee to keep the PS awake on return journey.

I drove the Permanent Secretary back.
He yawned many times in the back of the car
Then to keep awake, he suddenly asked,
Did you have any lunch friend?
I replied looking straight ahead
And secretly smiling at his belated concern
That I had not, but was slimming!

Upon which he said with a seriousness
That amused more than annoyed me,
Mwananchi, I too had none!
I attended to matters of state.
Highly delicate diplomatic duties you know,
And friend, it goes against my grain,
Causes me stomach ulcers and wind.
Ah, he continued, yawning again,
The pains we suffer in building the nation!

So the PS had ulcers too!
My ulcers I think are equally painful
Only they are caused by hunger,
Not sumptuous lunches!

So two nation builders
Arrived home this evening
With terrible stomach pains
The result of building the nation
   -different ways.

The leader that hung

When love and trust from the people he led
Flowed to him and warmed his heart, and
When he, in turn, loved and trusted his people
He blossomed and was magnificent.
But one day that Cancer of Suspicion
Within his heart was roused from its light sleep.
In the fertile soil of a leader's position
It was fed and it grew at an alarming rate.

One day Suspicion opened its sharp and ugly teeth
And gave Trust a deep and vicious bite.
Trust fought back with gentle pleading words
Beseeching the leader to throw out Suspicion.
But Suspicion, now grown into Fear, bit harder.
Trust spread his wings and flew out bleeding.
To fill his place vicious Hatred marched in
And joined his father in fatal attack.
Masters of their craft, they set to work.
They filled the leader's heart with crippling fear
Which flowed unhindered to the tips of his toes.
They turned his eardrum so it could hear
Lies where truth was spoken
And malice where none was meant.
They tinted his eyes so he could see
Cunning and intrigue in every soul;
His tongue they coated with sleek lies.
His thoughts were conditioned by an invincible
Craving ambition for absolute power for ever.

Love slowly bled to death
Forgiveness was starved
And Honesty slowly stifled.

But Fear, Suspicion and Hatred grew and grew.
They consumed his mind and sucked his blood.
Nothing was left of his former self.
The people he once proudly led, sadly
Shook their heads and in determined whispers said,
Our Leader is gone; this is not him.
We must hang this dangerous monster
Of Suspicion, Fear and unreasoning Hatred
Before it consumes us and our children
   And so they hanged their leader.

1969

Evenings on safari

The *Mugiini** stinks of bats
Like a stuffy old church.
The room empty, except for
A camp table and a matching chair,
A pressure lamp hissing,
Emitting light and a lot of heat.
And I, lonely, seated on the camp chair.
A bat flies in,
Hits the opposite wall
Squeaks and flies in,
Hits the opposite wall
Squeaks and flies out.
I shift in the camp chair;
It is so uncomfortable!
A beetle hits me in the face
Falls on the floor and
flies away again.
I turn a page,
A moth settles on my nose
I blink and blindly hit out.
It flies and hits the lamp,
Falls on the table
Flapping its clumsy wings,
Settles on the page.
I curse, shut the book
To crush it, but it flies.
It flies round and round
and round and round the lamp
And falls onto the table.
BANG! I miss it
BANG! another miss

Bang! Bang! Bang!
Down goes the spirit bottle.

BANG!
There is a mess on the book.
My God what a beautiful thing!
"A thing of beauty is a joy for ever
Its loveliness ..."
But I have killed it!
Smashed it!

1958

*Mugiini is or used to be a shutterless simple rest house in which government field officers used to camp on duty safaris.

The bullock

His role: servile service!
The uncomplaining whipping-boy.
His reward: meagre grass
And decorated harnesses!
Castrated in mind and body
He continues the Farmer's
Faithful servile servant
Forever led by his pierced nose!

Of feathers and dead leaves

Feathers and dead leaves
Ride the chaotic cataracts
Brushing against fierce boulders
And sharp ledges unscathed.
Not so for more substantial cargo.
Caught in the blind fury
Of the impulsive current,
With navigational skills
Impetuously discarded,
The boulders take their toll;
Smashed skulls
Broken ribs
And gash wounds.
In this accursed turmoil
Stubborn Hope keeps winking,
Giving us faith that one day
We may lick our wounds
And mend our fractured jaws
Beyond the cataract,
Beyond the rage.

Craving for dawn

Our frightened whispers
Echo from trunk to trunk
Like the anguished bellow
Of a trapped bull
In this weird forest.

But the mighty lords of darkness
Stride the forest confidently
The heavy crunch of their foot-falls
Sending paralysing tremors of fear
Into our crouched bodies.

They clean their deadly claws
Leaving dripping blood
On the violated barks
And the smell of warm blood
In the already fetid air.

Our lips are paralysed
And the vocal cords rigid with fear.
Our silent prayers have not hastened
The sweetness and light of dawn.

Yet we know
Dawn will come.
Dawn will come,
As will another night.

The ride to Chichicastenango

Chichicastenango!
The mystery, the music!
Chichicastenango.
The boring guide
Like a lifeless tape
Went on and on!
Antigua -
Victim of multiple earthquakes -
Fire-throwing volcanoes,
Dead volcanoes.
Lake Atitcan.

Ahead, a police motorcyclist,
Followed by a pick-up full of
Disguised armed soldiers
And behind, more police,
Somewhat dimmed
The music and charm
Of Chichicastenango!

All this; but to me,
The ride to Chichicastenango
Shall always remain
The violent excitement
That ate into my stomach
As I drank in the simplicity,
The beauty and the peace
Of the simple mountain people
In strife-torn Guatemala!

Here in the country,
In the mountains,
Life went on.

The people, the real people
Thatched their houses
And tended their maize
Celebrated marriages
And cried for their dead.

And in Chichicastenango
The priest of the Indian religion
Shared the Roman Catholic church
And a common congregation
With the garbed Reverend Father!

To crown the wonderful ride
To Chichicastenango,
From a fly-covered small girl,
Yellow mucus peeping from her nose,
I bought the most gorgeous
Exotic mauve and white wild orchids!

8 December 1971

Chichicastenango revisited

Maybe the fly-covered girl
Still smiles and sells exotic orchids;
And the two priests still share
The brick-red Catholic church
And the incense-burning congregation!

Maybe the simple people
In the Guatemala mountains
Still thatch their mud houses
Tend their small maize patches
Celebrate their marriages
Cry for and bury their dead,
Even when gun-brandishing gangs
Roam their beautiful mountains
Continuing the never-ending struggle
For transient political power!

From where I am seated,
Halfway across the world,
I again ride to
Chichicastenango
I again get butterflies in the stomach.

But in addition to the excitement
That ate into my stomach then,
There is also terrible terror.
I sadly realise that in the apparent
Peace I so much loved
They too had hidden terrors.
I ruefully realise that
Life must go on notwithstanding
The senseless struggle for power
Which is Uganda's fate now!

1973

The interrupted dream

I'll get drunk tonight
Four double waragis
In Fanta Ginger Ale
Quickly gulped down
Then a triple waragi - neat.

I'll then go to Twilight Bar
Where my boss sits every night
At the second table on the left.
He'll be there grinning stupidly
Sipping double whiskies and water
His lust brimming eyes stripping
Every slut in Twilight Bar!

In my second-hand army boots
I'll stomp noisily to his table
And deliver a loud and powerful bang
On the table making all glasses jump
And frightening the wits out of my boss.
I'll tower above the small cocky man
Hypnotising him with the fury in my eyes.

His stupid moustache will quiver
And the lustful grin quickly disappear.
Burning with anger and revenge
I will bellow at the benumbed man
Calling him a skunk and nincompoop
A good-for-nothing son of a bitch,
A sluggard sleepy snail!

I'll beef him on the nose
Knock out his yellow false teeth
I will give a hefty twist

To his oversized left ear
And pull his prestige moustache;
Smash his bi-focal spectacles
And watch his tearful unseeing eyes!

Ha! ha! ha! ha! ha!
Oh! ha! ha! ...
What are you laughing at you fool?
Where is the file I asked for
Thirty bloody minutes ago?
Sir ... I ... Sir ... am Sir ...
You are sacked
Get the hell out of this office.

Chameleon, leopard and blue-headed lizard

Chameleons and leopards
Resemble in only one respect.
Leopards never change their spots,
While chameleons never cease changing
Hues to suit their environment.

As I stand watching you seated
In the glare of television lights
Nodding your small angular head
And licking your always dry lips
Demonstrating your admiration
Of every sentence he utters
Be it an insult, joke or utter stupidity,
I am reminded of a blue-headed lizard
Nodding its square-jawed blue head
As it basks in the warm morning sun!

I smile to myself as I recognise
How constant we two have been.
One is a chameleon;
The other a leopard.

Of fawning dogs and purring cats

The fawning dog,
Tail between its legs,
Whimpering and whining
Shamelessly seeking a pat
On the back from the master!

The deceitful cat,
Rubbing its mistress's legs
With its soft smooth fur
Purring with apparent love
But in fact shamelessly begging
For food!

I despise fawning dogs
And flattering cats;
But worse still - *you*.
For when you grovel and flatter
And almost lick his fancy shoes
So you can prove your loyalty,
I see the fawning dog
Tail between its legs
And listen to the purring
Of a hungry cat pretending loyalty!

Ofttimes you are even worse!
Consenting, for the sake of an ephemeral pat,
To tasks you know to be
Impossible or stupid
And later blaming failure
On those you should protect!

Paper napkin
(for Daudi)

When after giving of your very best
You are crumpled like a used napkin
And thrown into a garbage bin
Pray do not attempt to resist
Or stick on their filthy fingers.
They will tear you to pieces
And even incinerate you to boot!

Rather, celebrate and shout with joy;
For humbler tasks like growing broilers
Or looking after your hogs in a pigsty
Will reward you with more joy and peace
Than helplessly listening to the speech
That cost you a sleepless night,
Researching, drafting and polishing,
Falsified and murdered by a fool
To cover his indolence and stupidity!

Bear the fools and the stupid kindly

Sheep, all sheep!
That's the problem.
Herds and herds of sheep
Blind stupid
Thoughtless followers
The whole lot of us!
Fools that can be led
To jump off sheer precipices
Completely incapable of
Realising the consequences.
Blockheads that are led
To scream slogans for years
The meanings of which
They never thought about
Even for a second.
Just stupid thoughtless fools
Following unquestioningly.
That is the biggest problem; or is it?

Imagine, for just one moment,
That each one of us
Was a cantankerous
Original thinker,
Bold enough to practise
Our individual, often stupid
And selfish idiosyncracies
What chaos, WHAT CHAOS!

So bear the fools and the stupid:
The unthinking blind followers, kindly.
Maybe they too contribute to some sanity
In our already troubled humanity!

29 June 1992

Uganda

(With apologies and deep appreciation to Walter de la Mare for creating 'Arabia')

Painful are the thoughts of Uganda
Where now Nuba rules in blood
Amidst silent and pained anguish
Under her glorious skies.
Dark are the hearts of her people
That cheer the princes of Nuba
Riding armoured troop-carriers,
Rattling, in midnight gloom.

Poignant earlier memories ...
They haunt me - the people, the country
The cheering green of inviting hills
The splendour of cloud-wrapped mountains
The mischievous giggle of youthful streams
And the quiet serenity of blue lakes
The roar of ever-thundering waters
And the silence of vast shimmering plains at noon.

They haunt me -
The beauties of my country haunt me
The black depth of star-filled skies
And the moon-silvered banana leaves
The bird-song-filled mists of dawn
And the smiling farewells of sunset colours
The pent-up anger of thunderstorms
The dark awe of impenetrable forests
And the billowing waves of grasslands.
They haunt me - my people haunt me.

The abandon of their happy laughter,
The twinkling friendliness in the eyes
Of naked children smiling at strangers.
The vain extravagance of the weddings
And the strangling poverty of the villages
The compassion and generosity at funerals
And the callousness and cruelty of *kondos*.

And oh! those drums - those bewitching drums!
The drummers' flitting hands flirting shamelessly
Tickling the responding tautness of the skin
The suppleness of suggestive waists
Flowing effortlessly from the unmatchable
Rhythm of agile feet in the dust!
The Bwola, the Dingi-Dingi, the Nankasa
It haunts me - her music haunts me!

Painful are the memories of Uganda
Where mercenaries plunder
They have slaughtered our guts through.
But one day our guts shall sprout
The broken bones shall mend
And the festering wounds shall heal.
Uganda once again shall be a smile!

1978, Ethiopia

Kondos: armed thieves

Fifty four

Amidst the bustle and commotion
The excitements and frustrations
Of launching the State ship again!

A few skilled gnarled hands
Plenty of untried enthusiasm
And the ship battered but undaunted.

Debating destinations
Charting intricate courses
Patching sails and stocking scanty provisions.

This time well aware of the unseen
Incomprehensible, often invincible
Undercurrents the dear ship faces.

This time fully aware of the fickleness,
Of the unpredictable squalls,
The shifting sandbanks of my native sea.

This time my hopes well tempered
With experiences of high personal costs
And the thanklessness of the task.

Whence then this great faith?
This irresistible surge of hope?
This determination and even excitement

At fifty four?

May 1983

Summit fever I: Father to son

My son!
You were born among the rolling plains
Where the ever-playful wind
Plays hide-and-seek in the supple grass
Caressing and tickling it into joyous laughter;
Where herds of cattle leisurely wander
Collecting the sweetness of the grass
Into the benevolence of their udders;
Where lambs and calves
Frolic in the dewy grass.

You were born under the wide blue skies
Where hilarious clouds race each other
Across the vastness of the horizon,
Where in the evenings, when the stars
Have burnt and perforated glowing holes
In the thick black cloak of night,
Homestead fires glow dotted across the land
- Imitation of the stars in the silent sky!

From the plains you have watched
The indolent waking up of the sun
How lazily it throws its numerous arms
Onto the sleeping hills around
And then tickles awake
The drowsy clouds of the eastern skies.

You often were astounded by the luxurious yawn
Of the exhausted sun in the evening
When it rubbed its drowsy red eye
And donned its crimson evening dress

Across the greying western horizon.
Many a morning you've woken up
By the glorious orchestra of bird songs
Hailing the Sun-God at dawn.

You have praised the beauty
Of the elegant white egret
Picking ticks off the browsing cows
And the majestic courtship-dance
Of the graceful Crested Crane.

Have you forgotten the forlorn cry
Of the silvery-green Ibis searching
For her lost children?

You also have known
The rigours of the plains
The trembling anger of the mid-day sun
Which causes all plants, in defeat,
To bow their heads and plead for mercy,
And the animals to chew their cud
Under the hushed trees and silent bushes.

You have often trudged weary miles
On paths of searing-hot brown dust
For a small pot of precious muddy water.

The wide shallow floods of the rainy season,
The sticky quagmires,
The hordes of irritating flies
The bloodthirsty mosquitoes
All this and much more my son!
But .... But .... this is life!

This is life as it was meant to be
The lowly plains are bursting with life!
The joys and sorrows
The beauty and ugliness
The ruthlessness and tenderness
The laughter and tears
These are the real essence of life!
The plains are bursting with life.
In comparison, the summit,
Your abode,
Is stone dead.

I have come to rescue you;
I have come to take you home!
To take you back to the plains and to life.
Away from your cold and bleak summit!

I know my son
The summit is an honoured and lofty place
The highest and the ultimate.
But it is also a weird and sinister place
It certainly is no place
For a prolonged and happy stay;
For its glories and joys
Are precarious and short lived.

The stay at the summit
Should be as long as an arrow's flight
From the twanging bow to receiving earth!

Come down, do not overstay;
For a mistress that tenaciously clings
Onto her capricious lover
Quickly blots out the tender rays of love
And loses what she best wanted to retain!

The summit was meant
For a short glorious stay
When it is fully bathed
In the pure sunshine of love
Of the humble dwellers of the plains.

When the weather changes
The summit is a deadly place.
The vicious gales of jealousy
And the sinister clouds of intrigue
Will most surely wreck any Lord of the Summit

The glare of publicity flashlights
Destroy the once-sensitive eardrums.

The stiff-necked protocol
Insulates one from the human touch
And all of these develop into Summit Fever
Which finally ends up in mountain madness!

Summit Fever is a cruel disease
A killer disease that does not kill
But gradually alienates you from your own;
Ostracizes and makes a leper of you.

People talk and converse with you
But only with their lips not their hearts
They will laugh with you, whilst laughing at you.

Summit fever is a killer that does not kill
A cat that plays with the dazed lizard
Postponing the inevitable tortured end.

I have seen the symptoms of the fever
In you my son!!
It must be the fever
If you cannot see,
As you do not now,
How your henchmen organise
The rabble to raise their hands
And scream at the mention of your name.

It does not surprise me
If you cannot hear,
As you cannot now,
The empty-tin-hollowness
Of their meaningless Oye! Oye!

It must be the fever
If, in your growing conceit
You mistake all this for loyalty
And wide spread love for you.

As for your trusted colleagues!!
Can sycophants ever be colleagues!?
What genuine advice can they give you
If whenever they open their mouths
They switch on recorded tapes of your speeches
To which they add monotonously,
Their one song of songs:

"Great is the Lord of the Summit
His wisdom knows no limits
He is forever in the right
His rule is forever and ever
Amen."

Come back to the lowly plains my son,
Let me take you back to sanity and life
Do not hesitate. Come now
Before it is too late!

Summit fever II: Brother to brother

Father went back disappointed!
I had tried to explain;
But what do you tell a man
Who thinks you are going mad?
Well, I am really stuck
On this accursed summit
I only hope I shall not end up
On some remote foreign plain with
A broken heart and broken spirit!

Father thinks I am blind;
That I cannot clearly see
The waning loyalty and love
Of the people on the plains.
Father thinks I am unaware
Of the jealousies and intrigues
To knock me off the summit.
Father thinks I am power-drunk.
He thinks I am really going mad
And I know he is not alone
Other independent minds think so!
Maybe you too, brother!

Well, you are all wrong.
I am perfectly within my senses
I am conscious of all things around me
And know much more than
You or father can ever know.

Brother!
Sometimes I boil with anger and cry
In the privacy of the friendly night

At the injustice of it all.
I have served this country
And selflessly given of the best in me.
Is it my fault that some of them
Have been more alert and energetic
And others indolent in gathering;
That some have snatched from the weak
And others are downright fools!

Brother,
Father entreats me to go back to the plains
He does not know I have considered doing just that
Many long nights and weary days.
Truly brother often I have almost decided
To shed this self-imposed crushing burden
For which I earn only callous ingratitude,
Unreasoning hatred and jealousy.
I have often concluded there is no reason
Why I should strenuously burn up
My fast dwindling reserves of energy
Helping uncomprehending, stupid,
Ungrateful and chaotic herds of sheep.
Why should I be the self-appointed
Guardian angel of the stupid flock?

Why not let the ignorant fools choose
Some power hungry upstart to lead them?
Why not let these snarling wolves in sheep skins
Fight it out and tear both themselves
And my beloved people to pieces?
Why not just let go?

But then, I always recognise with shock
That the stupidity of sheep,

Is an innocent type of stupidity;
That I should accept them as they are
For they were meant to be led or pushed;
And it is the shepherd's responsibility
Whether they go the right or wrong way.
I recall my avowed promises to them,
To lead them to more succulent pastures.

I begin to question myself
Am I a shameless deceiver who swore
Empty promises to my constituents?
Am I a cowardly deserter
Who turns tail and surrenders
At the first encounter of uninformed
Biased and unreasoning resistance?
I debate time and again with myself;
Has democracy a philosophy
Of firm and confident leadership?
Or is it a blind, slave-like execution
Of the wishes of the unenlightened masses?

I have concluded and with reasons
That a leader must lead! and sometimes
Overlook the wishes of his people
Where the terrain being traversed
Is unfamiliar to the flock he leads,
Thus I am imprisoned at the summit
By my convictions and sense of duty
By my avowed but unfulfilled promises.
You may ask, as father tried to,
After I had explained all this,
Whether I am not the most conceited man alive.
What evidence, what right have I
To consider myself the only arbiter

Of what is good or bad for the nation?
I am compelled to stay at the summit
To complete the wonderful projects
I have initiated with such effort
Which some braggart of an upstart
Will surely claim if I climb down.
No I cannot abdicate now.
I am not a coward. I will weather the storm.

Brother you now know why I cannot leave
The summit abruptly now.
I am a prisoner at the summit
With strong fetters at every turn.

When I had confided all this
To my brother, he was silent for a long time,
His eyes were downcast avoiding mine.
When he at last looked at me,
He said in a very sad voice,
Maybe father was right after all!
I then knew that he too was against me.
He rose without a word and left the room.
I have not seen my brother since!

Summit fever III: Epilogue

I now live in a humble bungalow
In the sweltering heat of a foreign plain
Nursing my bruised heart and broken spirit

I sadly recall my father's last visit
And the long talk I had with my brother.
Bitter tears roll down my cheeks
For the slaughter and bloodshed
Those power-drunk former colleagues,
Army officers and their lackeys
Have caused, and continue to inflict
On the people I've loved and served
And for whom I sacrificed everything

Two questions for which I have no answer,
Continue to haunt me unceasingly:
Can one ever fully understand
All there is in a situation
In which one is not totally involved?
Can one retain the love and loyalty
Of the people one leads, for all time
Without sacrificing truth and principles?

It continues to rain and the grass is greener

When I am getting too depressed
By my lacklustre achievements
I run to John Milton for comfort
Who on his getting blind wrote
"They also serve who only stand and wait!'

I rationalise my depressing failures
I repeat quietly to my woe-begone self
That nobody can start a bush fire
When it continues to rain all day
Or when the grass is young and green.

Match after match have I lighted
Without a great fire resulting!
The high hopes and aspirations
That fired my committed efforts
Are waning and being eaten away
While it rains on and the grass grows greener!

In these years of continuously recurring droughts
Which have caused terrible famines and suffering
How I wish for yet another great drought
To make this decaying growth of weeds
Tinder-dry for my tiny spark to burn the rot away!

When will this rain-drenched grass dry?
When will our time-barred efforts
Burst into a glorious and beautiful wildfire?
The match box is not inexhaustible
And may at any time suddenly dry out.

Or am I condemned to only stand and wait?

Jubilating South African democracy

I ululate with Desmond Tutu
For Mandela and all my black brothers
Who have struggled so long for release
From the cruel prison of apartheid
And now suffer a painful birth
Into the strange world of freedom!

I jubilate and shout with joy
For our white brothers too;
Who may at last liberate themselves
From the self-imposed slavery of fears
To the inevitable reality and truth
Of the strains of living together.

Yet at the back of my joy-filled eyes
I feel the painful sting of suppressed tears
Tears of great joy and great sadness;
For how many will embrace and accept
This newly found freedom, this democracy,
With understanding and compromise?

How many will suffer and even die
At the very same clapping hands
Of the now jubilating democrats
And those crying for the demise of apartheid?
Yet notwithstanding what may happen
I jubilate and ululate with hope!

For it is given to all of us to bear
The sharp pains of birth; and can not escape
The numerous growing pains and fears
Nor the tremendous joys and hopes
Until we attain sober maturity.

So let us make merry and celebrate
This momentous birthday!

2 May 1994

PART II

THE JUNGLES OF HUMANITY

Vietnam

Since my mother's leathery breasts
Grew cold in my toothless mouth
When a French bullet released her
From caring for her bastard son,
Tears have relaxed my tense existence
More than the rare occasions of laughter!

Salty rivers bathed my dusty cheeks
When the ever-present whine
Ended with a cold thud
In my grandma's weary head.
I cried floods then.
But now I am dry-faced
As I hold her lifeless in my arms!

Tears refuse to flow
To soothe my unseeing eyes
For I am now a ghost with a body
I am only a living corpse;
For this my life companion,
This my only surviving love
Does not answer when I call.
'Why do you stare unblinkingly Phon-Hue?
Where is that courageous smile
That has comforted my frightened existence?
Oh! Ye many-eyed gods
Tell me from where this piece of lead,
Picked out of her shattered head,
Was commandeered for its deadly mission.
Is it of a Peking make?
Did it fly from Viet Cong guns?
Was it made in Detroit?

Or is it made in Moscow?
Is it from the Village Guard's gun
Whose trembling hand shoots at shadows?

Speak out, thou tongue-tied gods
For once loosen your tongue and speak,
But better still pluck out of me
This over-blown sorrow
That will not allow me to cry
And plant it deep in the hearts
Of Chairman Mao Tse Tung
Richard Nixon in White House
Bearded Ho Chi Minh
And South Vietnam's Ky.
For they have never cried their eyes dry
And they have never known what sorrow is.
But they spread the venomous causes
Speaking with artificially impassioned voices
About vital principles I do not comprehend,
Of universal happiness and eternal peace
When Victory is won;
While I cannot cry -

    Not even cry.

The jungles of Biafra

The command was crisp and clear
Fight the rebel and bring unity;
Fight so the country may emerge
Strong, united and prosperous.

So the soldier marched into Biafra
Where the rebel was encamped.
He saw with unbelieving eyes
His tall bosom friend Fulani
Fall with a bullet in his neck.
He held dying Fulani in his hands
And heard with anguish and terror
Fulani's dying breath frothing in the windpipe
Through the red warm blood.

Forward the Command rang!
Kill or you'll be killed!
Fight for love, unity and peace!
There can't be unity without death!

But with Fulani's dying eyes
Staring blankly at him
And his frothy breath in his ears
It was not for the declared cause
He rose at brisk command.
Vengeance had taken over command
Anger supplied the fuel
Terror drove him blindly.

Like a wounded buffalo
He tore through the Biafran bush
On and on not knowing whither he went.

Tense, blind and frightened
He lunged forward through the bush
Clutching his gun so tightly
That his hands grew numb.

Exhaustion finally brought him to his senses
He found himself alone
And knew not where he was.
Then every simple jungle noise
Every windy movement of a branch
Was a rebel stalking him.
Would it be a Biafran spear?
Or the swift merciless bullet
That would pierce his throat?
From bush to thicket he crawled
With every muscle in his body
As tense as the highest string
Of the harp he left at home.
He knew not whither he was heading.

Suddenly in a shady clearance
He saw a child, a boy of five
Sitting playing with twigs.
There in the shady clearance
The boy took a twig
Held it firmly against his
Naked right shoulder
Aimed with studied coolness
At the bush that hid the soldier.

The soldier took a cool aim.
Shoot to kill, the trainer had said.
Kill for unity; kill for peace;
The Commander had said.

The enemy was within range
And was shooting at him.
It went through the small head
And the twig gun fell down.

Out of a bush a mother ran
To her son now dead.
She got it in the chest.
Out of the same bush came
A curse obscene and pure
From a voice aged and trembling.
The soldier sprayed the bush
With bullets, with the terror
The anger, the vengeance and fear
That had gripped him for so long.

Then suddenly trembling uncontrollably
His hand dropped the gun;
Tears streamed down his cheeks
And he sobbed like a child.
For a moment there was unity
Unity in his tense heart;
He had shot the enemy;
He had avenged Fulani.
There was peace in his soul.
But this peace was no peace
This unity was short-lived
For out of the bush he'd sprayed
So thoroughly with bullets
An old white-bearded man crawled
Dragging his bleeding shattered leg.

Shoot, coward shoot, he shouted.
For I have nothing to live for now.

Shoot for you are already dead and lonely
Dead, frightened and lonely
And you long for the company of the dead
For unity, peace and a new lease of life.

And there were heart-rending sobs
From where the Soldier lay writhing
For Vengeance had evaporated
And Anger gone, only Terror remained!
The Commander was far away
And the Soldier was alone
A frightened lost child in the jungle
   ... the jungles of Humanity.

The flight

He fastened his seat belt with trembling hands,
Took an involuntary breath and closed his eyes
To block unmanly tears demanding release.
But, with deep emotion, his huge body
Shook uncontrollably and warm tears
Rolled into his handsome black beard.

The soulless machine slowly gathered speed
Hurtled across the dusty pot-holed strip
And rose unconcernedly above the trees.
He looked out and through his tears saw
The land he loved, the land he knew so well
Fast receding, perhaps never to be seen again.
Suddenly immediately below him he saw
A group of three mushroom-shaped huts,
And out of one a starving boy staggered out
And with his thin hand waved goodbye!

He jumped from his seat as if stung
And in long soldiery steps strode to the cockpit.
With tears rolling down his distorted face
He bellowed, in agonised frenzy.
Turn back man, turn back.

The plane rose sharply and droned on.
Turn back, I command you. Do you hear?
A sudden feeling of helplessness gripped him
And clutching both sides of the cockpit doorway
Sickening sweat slowly oozed in his armpits
And rolled like iced water drops
Down the sides of his heaving chest.
Drops of sweat quickly formed on his brow
Mingled with his streaming tears and rolled
Into his black-as-ebony beard.

The pilot slowly turned his grim face
And confronted the defeated leader.
Sympathy for the leader, responsibility and fear
Had also distorted his professionally calm face.
With deliberate calmness he quietly said,
It is dangerous for you to stand there,
Take your seat and fasten your seat belt.
Boarding this plane you abdicated your Authority.

Odumegwu Ojukwu was stunned!
His heels automatically clicked to attention
And he drew himself to his full noble height
To reprimand the insubordinate pilot.
But suddenly he felt dizzy and sick
And stumbled blindly to the nearest seat,
And his huge body shook with sobs.
In his already embroiled mind teeming questions
Continued their detached and unmerciful
Tearing and dissection of the man.

Am I a coward? Am I running?
Is this a tactical retreat?
Or is it ignoble defeat?
Is this the end?

The plane hit a rising air pocket
Rolled slightly and steadied
And droned unconcernedly out of Biafra.

30 October 1970

PART III

ARGUMENTS WITH GOD

The image of God

Was the clay unmalleable?
Or could it be that
Godly hands faltered?
For if it weren't that,
Then surely God is not
What we imagine He is;
Or man was fashioned
After the devil, not God!

God is magic

Daddy when you die,
Said Philippa innocently,
We shall have no Daddy.
And when Mummy dies,
We shall have no Mummy.
When you both die
Where will you have to go?
I've forgotten, tell me Daddy.
Daddy said, I do not know.
To heaven, said Philipa
With glee, having remembered,
Because Daddy, God is magic
and Jesus is Magic.
Isn't He Daddy?

25 March 1969

Argument with God

My child was struggling for life in hospital,
And I, worried tense and tired,
Sat in silent prayer;
In violent silence arguing with God.

God, I said,
Why do you allow him to suffer so?
Why him all the time?
Why?
God was silent!
Not a word from him,
Not a word.

Maybe, I thought,
God is angry with me.
I'll appease my God,
Promise Him to be good.
God, I pleaded,
Please God,
I am not a good man,
But I'll try to be
    ONLY,
My child must live;
Live free from pain.

God, I continued,
You know how I love him don't you?
Don't you, don't you, DON'T YOU?
    But,
God was dumb.
Dumb, like my child.

Then I said to myself,
God is just.
I'll appeal for justice.
He cannot deny me justice.
God I called,
Though you are silent,
I am sure you hear me.
Be fair, be just,
Let him live strong and happy.

Then,
I saw on the wall,
A cockroach pregnant with egg,
In the pains of labour,
Bringing forth new life.
I snatched a newspaper,
And hit the cockroach.
It fell on its back,
Struggling for life,
And I crushed it,
With the heel of my shoe.

All the time I was praying,
Violently pleading for life.

1967

An honest prayer to God

God:

If you do exist,
For I am in dilemma if you do,
Then scoop out the dregs
Of your much vaunted mercy
And pour it onto me!

Hah!

But what prayer is this?
How can God respond to this,
My anguished shriek, couched
As it is, in sarcasm and doubt;
Meant to be an honest solicitation
But bristling with pained anger and pride?

The half-witted street beggar is sure
Of some kind donors' existence.
But I am doubtful of His,
To whom I address this plea!
How then can this be a prayer?
How can one plead with Void?

Yet God,

If you do exist after all,
And these my tribulations
Are one of your mysterious ways
To bring me back to the fold ...

Fold indeed!

What a humbling expression!
Do you really want us, God,

As a herd of docile stupid sheep?
Honestly God,

If you want me back into camp,
Is this the way to do it?
For if you strip me naked
Of my self-respect and confidence
And leave me a snivelling spineless worm
Cringing with suffering and anxiety,
Of what value shall I be to you?
Or for that matter to my fellow men?

Surely,

If your bountiful and tender mercies
Were showered upon me
You would most certainly win me over
And I would come to you with
My chin held high and chest out
Able to thank you and be militant in your praise.

Yet,

I must honestly admit
That too often in my moments of joy
I've forgotten even the shadow of your presence!

Therefore Lord,

Doubtful, proud, and rebellious as I am
Let me humbly say
Thy will be done!

6 January 1976

Crucifixion

Jesus,
Once long ago you died
- only once -
Upon a cross.
You rose from the dead
And since then
You have sat in heaven
On a golden throne
And watched -
And watched us die
Not once not twice
But several times over!

I have died several times
Only to rise and then
Die and rise again.
I must be a cat
And a super-cat at that!

But you died only once
And your death was majestic -
An explosion of publicity.
Even to-day, nearly
Twenty centuries since,
Your death is celebrated
Every hour round the world!

There were milling crowds
Demanding and jubilating
Your death;
You even had company -
Albeit they were thieves!

But I die alone
- always alone!
In anguish and loneliness -
Albeit self-imposed loneliness.

I teach no principles
That would excite a crowd
To demand and jubilate my death.
I do not attract animosities;
I am too frail for that
And yet l am crucified
Over and over again!
By accidental frailties
And I die -
Alone.

Yet Lord, in truth,
I've never really died alone!
I have screamed for you
And often felt your compassionate hand
On my fevered brow;
And my loved ones have always been there -
Albeit on their crosses too!

Lord!
I do not crave for publicity
Or pomp for my re-occurring deaths!
Who, except you, can bear
Even one public crucifixion?

No!

It is the excrutiating pain
And the numerous bouts of deaths
For no explicable reason

That I quarrel with you about.
Can't you grant me
One single death at the end of it all -
Be it ever so humble and insignificant?

24 November 1979

Palm Sunday 1985

Yesterday these four young palm trees
Were singing and jubilating in the wind
Perhaps praising the good God
For the coming of the rains after the drought!

This morning, looking like half-plucked,
Dishevelled and dejected chickens,
In motionless anguish and silent anger
They mourn the violent assault Christianity
Has inflicted on their beautiful feathers and limbs.

Of what significance was the carrying
Of a palm leaf to any of the assailants?
Was it the instinct of the herd?
Did it add one iota of spirituality to any of them
This Palm Sunday?

Tussling with truth

I visited Truth for I admired him
I so much wanted to be friends with him.
I looked Truth straight in the face.
He had fathomless beautiful eyes!
Deep-sunken and mysteriously penetrating.

I asked Truth to be friends,
Truth and I.
His piercing eyes roved over me
And I felt naked before him.
He then said quietly,
It takes two to make friends.
How can we be friends,
You and I,
When you befriend me
Only when it suits you?

Ah! said I,
More lightly than I felt,
But it is all your fault!
More often than not
You are so disconcerting.
In fact, at times,
You are positively against me.
How do you expect me then
To constantly stand for you?

Truth smiled sadly
And said with a sigh
So you too think
It is me who is at fault!

Of course it is your fault!
I said, having heard Truth complain
That others thought so too.
Let me tell you
A few home truths about yourself.
You are so conceited!
You insist
That whoever should be your friend
Must accept your principles absolutely
But you accept nothing from him.
What friendship is yours
Lacking any give-and-take?
You are a dictator, an absolute dictator!
You do not listen to anyone.
Why do you really believe
Others have no good in them?
What is so good about you anyway?
You have no feelings, no sympathy
No consideration whatsoever.
You treat the strong and the weak,
The great ones and the scum of the World,
The saintly and the demons exactly the same.
But then, incomprehensibly to me,
You are at one and the same time
So fickle and unreliable!
You can be so sweet and felicitous
Sometimes you caress and comfort,
But often in no time at all
You are hard, stern and merciless,
To the same person you were comforting!
You are sometimes so unbelievably cruel
Absolutely shattering and destructive!

Truth looked at me with a touch of contempt
If I am that, then why seek my friendship?
Why not shun me and save yourself
The shame of having such a fickle friend?

That jolted me and I looked at Truth
But I did not see him!
For where he had been sitting
Sat someone familiar but not Truth!
On his seat I saw a stranger.
His face was a puzzle
One side of his face was
Beautiful calm and kindly
The other was stern and hard.
He noticed my confusion
And said in a kindly voice
I am the one you want to befriend
I am Truth I am changeless and ageless
Maybe you know me a little better now!
Maybe we shall be friends sometime someday!
But are you sure you want me for a friend?

PART IV

RANDOM PORTRAITS

Portrait of a young girl

I never knew her -
Not even her name!
But I testify truthfully
Her every step shouted
Look at me.
Look at me!

As she gracefully passed by
Men's eyes audibly whispered
Beautiful beautiful beautiful!
The smile on her face acknowledged;
Whispered back with shameless glee
I've heard what you've said

You are telling me
What I already know!

Nnasuuna the country girl

A dahlia once grew in the shade
Of a beautiful big tree.
Denied of the toughening rays of the sun
I watched its frustrated struggle to grow.
Long after other dahlia in the sun
Had filled the garden with gorgeous blooms,
And nectar-hungry busy bees
Were no longer dazzled by fading blooms,
The branch that robbed the little dahlia
Of the life-giving rays for so long
Was cut from the big shady tree.
One day therefore the little dahlia too
Burst into a long-awaited bloom.
It achieved no deep sun-rich colours
But the fragile paleness of its tints
Became the short-lived craze of the garden.
But the beautiful bloom was too heavy
For the shade-stunted little dahlia.
The stem gave way and the pale-tinted flower
Wilted slowly and sadly died before it could seed.

Nnasuuna was such a dahlia!
She came to town a simple country girl
Long after her sun-fed age-mates
Had bloomed with permed hair,
Exotic perfumes and shapely attire.
The bees loved her simple country ways
And the freshness of her small fragile body.
They buzzed around her and hungrily
Sucked the country purity of her sweet nectar

She died alone in childbirth;
For the ways of the town were too much
For the simplicity of the country girl.

The singer

Chuho spring - life giving waters -
Gushes fresh pure and bubbling
Out of black burnt-out lava ash
Amidst stunted and lifeless bush.

Chuho spring - embodiment of life -
In the parched desert of lava ash
Flows fruitlessly away unused
By the thirst consumed scrub!

Like this life giving spring,
He, of whom I sing,
Stood amidst starving souls
And burst into a beautiful song;

Spontaneous, wild and irresistible.
His song was hauntingly beautiful
A source of new exciting life
To the starved and wilting souls around.

In a world of his own,
Oblivious of the dead crowd,
The traffic noise, and the rain,
He sang his heart out.

But the rain-trapped crowd, huddled
Under the Supermarket verandah,
Did not hear his wild song!
They had no hands to clap,
No legs to stamp the rhythm.

No voice to ululate and join in chorus
And enrich the story with dialogue;
Not even eyes to see the singer!
Only
Blind
Mute
Deaf
Limbless bodies vacantly staring
At the noisy traffic in pouring rain!

* Chuho spring is in Kisoro District Western Uganda.

Errand to Sibemalizibwa

The sun was bright that morning!
It seemed to be smiling in the sky,
But I, tense and frightened,
Pretending to be calm and composed,
Drove grimly to my inescapable errand.

I remember her vividly that morning.
She radiated youthful vitality that morning
Like the first full bloom of a dahlia
Waving lightly in a fresh morning breeze
When first the sun kisses its dewy petals:
That was how I found her that morning.

Her hair, beautifully made,
Seemed alive like the grass in the wind.
Her dress reflected the youthful body it covered.
She was smiling when I came to her,
She was youth, she was a smile.

I seared the smile,
I killed the bloom
With the news I hated to utter.
In my hands I saw her shrivel
Like a weed plucked by the roots
And thrown irretrievably onto a fire.
I watched helplessly the fire gnawing
Right through her lovely body and soul
While I uttered meaningless cliches.
She is recovered now
And her age is not much changed
Her body is still beautiful
Her smile is charming still
But if you look closely
You will notice the scars
And the subtle damage of the news
I uttered that lovely morning.

My boss

Some bosses are tough all through;
Right from their heads to their toes!
Some are soft and smooth all through.
But comrades my boss is an enigma.
He is a soft comfortable cushion
For his bosses to sit on and relax.
My master has soft padded sides
That are a delight to his equals.
But his bottoms and his feet!
These are made of heavy cast iron.
He treads cruelly on us his underlings
And his heavy cast iron bottoms
Crack the heads of those who carry him.
His eyes are abnormal comrades.
Yours and mine can perceive clearly
Whether we look up or down
But my master's abnormal eyes
Can only see good when he looks up
And can only focus on faults
When they stare downward!
When he speaks to his bosses
His words are as soothing as velvet
But when he speaks to me - my God!
His voice drills holes in my ears.

His morphology is all wrong comrades
For he is soft in the head
But has heavy cast iron bottoms.

White lizards

They were not really white
Nor were they pink either!
A sort of unevenly bleached
And freckled pink if you wish.
Like monitor lizards on the lakeside,
They lay basking in the searing
And unrelenting mid-day sun.

They lay in all sorts of postures.
Some pornographic
Some exhibitionist
Some as if actually dead
Some strikingly enticing.
Once in a while
They'd jump into the pool
Splash and fool about
Then come out to bask.

But there was this odd one -
Black as soot and male to boot
Made all others as white as snow -
At least in comparison!
Apparently quite literate too!
- Reading a book lying on his back
In the fierce mid-day glare!
Or was he just attracting attention?
The sun-wisdom of his Africa
He had thrown quite overboard -
Basking in the searing mid-day sun!!

All these sun-crazed lizards
Lay basking in the searing
Unrelenting mid-day sun
Including the one black as soot
Who made all the others
    As white as snow.

Harare Sheraton, 1 May 1989

New York

I have heard and read
Exciting and eloquent eulogies
Of your unsurpassed beauty,
Your unmatched charms
They have sung of your
Vast treasures and variety
Of paintings and sculptures
From all over the world.
I have heard of Broadway
Wall Street, Central Park
Empire Building and Green Village
Harlem and its no-go joints.
I have longed to savour
All these at my leisure.
But every time I have visited you
Hoping and anxious to savour
All these your charms,
I have ended up only being teased
By the proximity and inability
To explore you, New York.
The few times I have visited you
I have arrived in penury
Calculating and recalculating
My small stock of dimes with which
To pay my board and lodging;
My time has been spent in boardrooms,
Stiff official dinners and small talk.

I fear you, you shall always remain
A mystery to me, New York.

Old Mousey

If you want to know why
I always called him Mousey,
Once in a flush of perception
I saw him and have done so since
As a sick old mouse I caught,
At the age when mice fascinated me,
In mother's sweet potato patch!

He was a grousy old cockney;
Or was he from Yorkshire?
Whatever he was anyway,
The only lively thing about him
Was his very tangy accent.
He was short and thin
With wide watery blue eyes;
Long melancholy greying whiskers.

He often wore khaki shorts
It was colonial fashion to do so.
But his were extremely wide-legged.
His emaciated hairy thighs
And knobbly-kneed legs stuck out of them
Feebly into faded khaki stockings,
Held upon his thin flabby calves
With red woollen garters.

I always found it funny he should smoke
for I do not think mice should;
But he smoked a foul smelling tobacco
From a short ugly-looking pipe -
Which probably accounts for the faint
Orange colour on his greying whiskers!

He once came to my office
Looking very mousey and old.
He raised his thin wasted leg
Upon the visitor's chair in front of me.
He was silent for a long time
Sucking at his ugly unlighted pipe
And suddenly burst out
Damn all university graduates
Why should they be paid higher salaries?

My C.S.D. (which stands for
Co-operative Secretary's Diploma)
Is higher or at least equivalent
To an MA from Oxford!

He was a product of Co-operative
Adult Education Evening Classes;
And now in the Colonial Service
He was a Provincial Co-operative Officer!
Poor Old Mousey!
His whiskers were so melancholy!

1978

Hanlon

He was a bull of a man
He never talked, he bellowed.
He was a Provincial Officer;
How could he not be?
He was such a good cricketer!

All week he ran the Province
Arranging nets, home
And away cricket matches;
Plus of course bellowing at
His cowered staff.

Excellent wicket-keeper;
He was so broad, no ball
However fast and wide
Would pass him by for a bye
But best of all, you ought to have heard
Him bellow, "HOW's ZAT?"

Once this young Indian school boy
From Kampala Secondary School
Kept piling ones and twos
With a very straight bat
And would not be got out.

Captain Hanlon had word with the bowler
Who delivered a very wide ball
Hanlon bellowed a tremendous HOW's ZAT?
The boy was so frightened he ran
From his crease and was stumped!
And the Umpire gave him out.

He however taught me one home truth
Conveying me to the district
Where I was posted under him,
He said young man you may be a graduate
But you know nothing about
The work you are going to do.
Some years later
I admitted to myself
What he said then was not
A racial prejudice as I took it.
It was very true then!

Meeting my soul-brother - Dulles Airport

I'll carry your luggage, sir,
My soul-brother asserted.
I begged his pardon,
For his twang was unfamiliar
And my mind was wondering
Whether home-town boy had come for me.
Am paid to help you sir,
Grabbing my almost empty suitcase
And on to his trolley confidently.
Recovering from the assault, I thought,
No need to object and explain
I had not changed money to pay him with.
He has said he's paid to help me!
And he is my long-lost soul-brother.
He is even darker than me!

Soul-brother leads the way
With slow straining steps
As if he was pushing a tonne.
I am irritated -
Same feeling as I get
Watching the taxi meter
Ticking and clicking away
In a long traffic jam.
But wait. He is paid!
So why worry?

Then I spy home-town boy.
He is just one broad welcome smile.
Relief. Good old Denis!
I rush to him. Hugs,
And greetings in home-town lingo.
At last, soul-brother arrives

Delivers the tonne of suitcase!
Thank you brother, I say,
Extending a hand of gratitude.
Three dollars sir,
Soul-brother snaps, ignoring
My hand extended in gratitude.
What?
I almost shout amazed.
Three dollars for pushing
Ten kilos unasked
For a mere fifteen meters?
Three dollars sir, he snarls.

But, meantime Denis has handed
Four dollars to soul-brother.
I fume.
Otherwise, your soul-brother,
Denis whispers to me,
Will remain convinced
That you sleep in a twig nest
In the dark twilight of
A thick African mahogany forest!

September 1966

Fay

I remember her walking to me
Slowly dragging her lame leg.
She stared long and sweetly into my eyes
and in her slow faltering way
She with radiant happiness said,
Taata nkuyagala nyo!
Greatly moved I drew her to my bosom
and in a whisper said: Bless you my love.

She still comes to me
With her love overflowing as ever
But now it is only her eyes and smile
That speak - perhaps more forcefully -
Taata nkuyagala nyo!

14 February 1970

My grandmother's eyes

I sat in front of a mirror this morning.
My grandmother's eyes stared straight at me!
They were there in that sheet of glass;
Deep-set piercing eyes
In sockets deeper than most.
I then knew whose eyes I see
When Hugo stares wide-eyed
Or when Betty's eyes flash with anger!

27 December 1968

Growing into a lizard

Staring wide-eyed into the mirror
Straining to shave below the chin
I saw a big lizard staring at me -
Wide-eyed with a very loose skin,
And a thousand wrinkles
Below its jaws and around its neck.
The lizard was shaving too!!
Laughter bubbled from my stomach
And I burst out laughing

1992

PART V

OF NATURE

Masaaba from Nkokonjeru

All was flat.

All was flat in the north and west;
And the roads like thin brown ribbons
Grew thinner and thinner and lost themselves
In the haze and mist far away.
Lake Kioga lay far in the west
Like a bed-sheet laid out to dry.
But in the South!

In the South and East how majestic!
The great mount rose from the plains
With indescribable splendour.
The foot hills like many-sided pyramids
Clothed in beautiful banana-green
Dignified the dark blue of the lofty range.
It soared so high that the clouds in anger
Of its approaching so near their abode
Swirled around the rocky peaks
Making a crown of white on the dark blue.

December 1951

Masaaba alias Mt. Elgon
Nkokonjeru is one of its ridges

Rainy morning

To have stayed in the warm
Cocoon of soothing sheets,
While the sulky and frowning
Clouds melted into a dull
Fretting and snivelling drizzle!

To have lain there curled
In a womb of comfortable warmth
Day-dreaming with closed eyes
Shutting out the burdens of the day
And this gloomy-faced morning!

To have quietly slipped into childhood
And listened again to the soft drumming
Of the raindrops on the banana leaves
And the lulling splash of tea-coloured water
From the old thatched roof!

To have basked warmly
In the comforting knowledge
That I could stay in bed
As long as I wanted!

But now I sit
In this cold Executive Chair
Against all my inclinations.

The death of an eland

Those eyes!
Those liquid green eyes
Tearless yet crying
Terrified and silent
Imploring for mercy
Those eyes haunt me.

We stood and looked at her
Emaciated with hunger and pain
Lying on her side, with the festering leg
Dripping with pus, held in the air
Trying in vain to heave herself up with her other legs.

Those eyes!
The terrified liquid eyes
Fervently transmitted pleas for mercy
And the body shook with terror and pain .
The emaciated legs kicked feebly
Trying to get her up
Where she had tripped and fallen.
There were ticks on her belly
Some were fat and bluish green
And there were numerous small brown ones.
The eyes begged!
Those haunting eyes.

The hunter said in a matter-of-fact way
It is kinder to shoot her
And raised his gun.
There was a kick and a feeble neigh
The body relaxed; the neck fell back.

The eyes looked at me
Still pleading
As if the hunter had not been merciful
And I stood there
Feeling foolish.
I noticed the ticks -
Still sucking.
I walked away
With liquid eyes
And followed the hunter.

Naked Meru*

The sun caught you completely naked
In deep silent sleep this morning!
Your soft white blankets
At the bottom of your green foot-hills.
Sun said: Wake up you lazy man!

You blinked your sleep-reddened eye
Smiled sleepily and briefly
Pulled up your blankets of cloud
Right over your rugged sleepy head
And went to sleep again!

All I can see of you now
Are your wide-spread green foot-hills
You lazy man!

* Mt. Meru in Tanzania

Laughter at death

The forest had ripened
Into a giant garden
Of gold, yellow and red.
The wind tickled the garden
Mischievously while the sun smiled.
The leaves laughed with merriment
Little realising their fate!

The wind tickled the leaves
And the leaves fell one by one;
In dozens they died
In ripened splendour.
Gently they were eased
Into the dark underworld.

The forest raised its naked
Arms to heaven in prayer
For a befitting burial.
God gently sprinkled
White dust and covered the graves
And he clothed the trees
In befitting black and white
While they silently mourned
The inevitable death of the leaves.

New York November 1983

Desirable war!

At last war drums and booming guns!
Militant clouds assemble in the sky
To fight the long incensed anger of the sun.
The leafless trees in ugly nakedness
Stand in earnest and silent prayers
The scorched grass flex their emaciated roots
Beneath the brown singed and cracked soil.
Even the restless wind stands motionless
Lest it blows the militant clouds away.
The buffalo dilates its wide dry nostrils
Sniffs the charged air for signs of victory.
A melodious chorus of encouragement
Ensues from the choking throats of birds
For the brave clouds to do battle and win!

26 March 1984

Rain at daybreak

Wind woke up first;
Got bored and restless
Sitting alone in the sky.
Wind decided to wake up the trees
And the grass, his usual playmates.
He flew among the tree leaves
And the tall elephant grass
Fondling and tickling them playfully.
The leaves giggled and screamed
Annoying fierce and ugly-tempered thunder.
Thunder lost his temper and bellowed SHUT UP
Released lightning and sparks
Right across the black sky
It was then that the black rain clouds
Bursting with loads and loads of rain
Saw Wind playing with the trees.
The rain clouds jumped onto Wind's bare back
And hung desperately on Wind's neck!
Wind screamed loudly 'cause the rain clouds
Were extremely heavy and dripping wet!
Wind screamed again and again.
Thunder, mad with fury, let off yet another
Most frightening thunderbolt and lightening
Which shook the whole wide sky.
For seconds dusky dawn was as bright as day.
The wetness on the rain clouds fell off
As a gentle shower onto the earth below.
Wind was frightened out of his wits
Sprinted right across the shaking sky
To hide from the angry and violent Thunder
In that blind and record-breaking sprint
The flimsy and overstretched bags

In which the rain clouds stored their water
Were torn and split by tree branches
Jagged rocky outcrops on hill tops.
And did it rain! It simply poured!
It poured. Thunder was nearly drowned!
He retreated to the periphery of the sky
Grumbling and mumbling until defeated
He became incoherent and then silent.
Lightning was snuffed out gradually
Sun was caught half awake in bed.
He blinked his eyes briefly and went to sleep!

PART VI

THE RICH LIVE AMALGAM

When I am dead and gone

When I am dead and gone
And in the brown earth am laid
Do not heap me with cold stones
And pray do not cement me in;
Don't rob me of the sweet warmth
Of the sun when it smiles
Nor of the cool fragrance
Of the breeze at dawn.
No. But let my bones feel
The warmth of the sun after rain
Let flowers grow on my grave
Let them wave and smile over me
As I have smiled on this world.

February, 1952

Uganda from Oxford

Grey dripping skies
Gaunt black buildings
Swallowing and vomiting
Vomiting and swallowing
    Restless ants!

Dull grey male ants
Bright clad female ants
Tall ants and short ants
Brisk ants and shuffling ants.

Everflowing
Multi-coloured
Multi-sized
Wheeled streams
Belching nauseating
Petrol fumes
Diesel fumes
White fumes
Black fumes;
Emitting weird noises
Deep low zooming noises
High ear-spliting noises
Groaning and stuttering noises.
Between these maddening streams
And the gaunt caverns of shops
    I walk!
Tottering grannies in front
Zigzagging the pavement
Blocking me left or right!
While their waist-coated dogs
Trip my tired wet feet!
Umbrella ribs threatening

To pluck my watering eyes out.
Teenage lovers bump me
As they shamelessly demonstrate
How fervently they can kiss!
Frock-coated newspaper vendors
Shouting eye-catching headlines.
Thin-legged teddy-boys
In dirty blue jeans
Wearing long female hair
Snigger at the weary nigger.
Amidst this motly bedlam
I walk.

Cold wailing babies
Mute freezing babies
In deluxe prams
Utility prams
Dingy pushchairs
Transmit secret messages
To the father in me,
While their mothers
Gossip in Marks and Spenser.
The heart twinges but
I walk on.
Both my arms nearly pulled
Out of their shoulder sockets
By our week's provisions.
Silently cursing
Visibly fuming
At the point of bellowing
Like a speared bull
I still walk on!

God! how I longed for my Uganda!

Winter 1959-60

The village well

By this well,
Where fresh waters still quietly whisper
As when I
First accompanied Mother and filled a baby gourd,
By this well,
Where many an evening its clean water cleaned me;

This silent well,
Dreaded haunt of the long-haired Musambwa,
Who basked
In the mid-day sun reclining on the rock
Where I now sit
Welling up with many poignant memories;

This spot,
Which has rung with the purity of child laughter;
This spot,
Where eye spoke secretly to responding eye;
This spot,
Where hearts pounded madly in many a breast;

By this well,
Over-hung by leafy branches of sheltering trees
I first noticed her.
I saw her in the cool of a red, red evening.
I saw her
As if I had not seen her a thousand times before.

By this well
My eyes asked for love, and my heart went mad.
I stuttered
And murmured my first words of love
And cupped,
Her heaving breasts with my trembling hands.

In this well,
In the clear waters of this whispering well,
The silent moon
With a smile witnessed our inviolate vows
And the kisses
That left us weak and breathless.

It is dark.
It is dark by the well that still whispers.
It is darker,
It is utter darkness in the heart that bleeds
By this well,
Where magic has evaporated but memories linger.

Of damp death
The rotting foliage reeks,
And the branches
Are grotesque talons of hungry vultures,
For she is dead;
The one I first loved by this well.

Eating alone

Me?
At table alone?
But didn't you see them
All of them around me?
Fay trying so hard with the food
And Chris refusing every dish?
Didn't you hear me shouting at Philly
To put her book away?
Didn't you hear Estella
Excusing herself for being late?
And didn't you hear Fayce telling Maliza
Not to leave all of us at table?
Didn't you see me grabbing
The biggest slice of the pawpaw?
And Fayce eating rice without sauce
When all of us had finished?
They were all there!
That's why I was so alone!

Addis Ababa, 1 December 1976

The bull

A bull's job
Is to service
Not to serve!
No docile ploughing
While whips cut
Into callous buttocks,
And metal nooses
Tear the sweating nose.
    Oh no!
That's bullocks' work.

Bullocks are disposed
To trudge the mulch
Churning it with ploughs;
To strain their backs
Pulling heavy cartfuls
Of blames and curses
That should be borne
By blundering whip-bearers.

This breed is no company for me
I cannot bear their muteness!
I have live balls -
Pendulums between my legs.
I long to bellow
And paw the ground,
Climb the beauty queen
of the herd
And have my fill.

This metal ring
I shall rip from my nose
And tear the harness asunder.
I shall break the yoke
And search for virgin pastures.
I must regain my freedom
From the mute silence of bullocks.

The horse

I have watched this horse
Trudge the same path
At the break of dawn
At the same pace
With the same gait
Day after day, day after day.

And the same small man
In a dirty kaftan
With bleary cruel eyes
And flabby silly lips
Has waved his swishing whip
And uttered the same commands.

The horse and the stunted man
Have gone round the gnarled tree
Skirted the jagged rock
Up the gentle slope
Past the deserted hut
To the old water wheel.

The corrugated horse stops.
The blank little man
Harnesses the horse
Shouts the same commands.
The horse shakes its weary head
And starts going round.

Plod ... plod ... plod ... plod
All day long plod ... plod.
No pause no change
And the blank little man
Always around and the whip
Providing encouragement!

And the leaking buckets
Come up, spill dirty water
Into the same trough
Down the disrepaired canal
Into the insatiable soil
And the hot dry wind.

And the horse goes
Round and round
Every day of the week
Every week of the year.
And I cry for the horse
And for this plodder too.

Tears for Taurus

I have searched over the whole wide pasture
Crept under every bush and thicket
Hoping that in this purulent epidemic
You had hid your mauled spirit low
Trying to nurse it in quiet solitude
But alas! I have not found you.

Where have you disappeared to
Source of my peace and confidence?
I cast my eyes where you used to walk
So calmly and confidently
Exhaling security, peace and happiness,
And I see puny mice running amok,
I seek wide-eyed hares paralysed,
Immobile, numb and helpless
Waiting for the hunter's knobbed club.

Have they at last broken your back?
Have they robbed you of your stubborn pride
And reduced you to the common herd?
Oh! my Taurus, my star
What foul ill-omened cloud
Hides you from my adoring eyes?
Why do you leave me unguided
Drifting rudderless on this turbulent sea?

No! I know you shall not desert me
They cannot break your back;
No passing cloud can extinguish a star!

1975

44

Forty four times
Have I helplessly
Orbited the fiery orb -
An undetected ant clinging
On an insignificant satellite
In the immensity of space!
Forty four juggler's rings
Jumbled and interlocked
Have I involuntarily gathered,
And do not know how many more
May interlock onto my cluster
Nor when the gathering hand
May lose its uncertain grip.

To what use these orbits,
These discordant rings?
Imperceptibly one circular orbit
Merges into an elliptical one
And the desperate ant clings on
Hoping one day to master
Its dizziness and gain
A sense of direction and purpose.
What direction?
And to which end?
Suffice it if a smile
May occasionally brighten this face
Like a tongue of pure flame
Unexpectedly shoots up
From the smouldering logs
Momentarily enlivening the dark hut.

Suffice it that once in a while
The heart should miss a beat
And the body stand arrested
Stunned in the beauty of a moment.
The immensity of Time and Space
have no salient landmarks
To lend searching Purpose
A gratifying goal to pursue.

So forty four years have gone by
and still the questions come
Who am I?
What purpose?
To what end?
To answers, like a swarm
of fireflies in the black night
Flash by, tantalisingly
Eluding capture
Perpetuating the fascination
of Life.

May 1973

49

Why mourn the victorious march of invading age?
Or its accompanying traits of diffidence and compromise?
True, time was when our postures were defiant
When our steps were bold and confident.
Problems released no butterflies of doubt
In the stomach, nor heartaches of indecision.
There was no pause between question and answer
No stunning pause when our minds
Recall cautioning failures and lurking dangers
Maiming the stature of imaginative and bold resolve.
We had precise answers unmarred by shadows of doubt
Ah! what a time, what a time that was.

Even then, why lament that which will never return?
Rather, we should rejoice and jubilate,
Chuckle quietly with ruminating glowing eyes
Ringed with mischievous radiating wrinkles -
Golden sunset rays of contentment after a glorious day.

Let our bodies shake with heart-felt laughter
As we recall those wild acts of daring youth
Those sure remedies, panacea of world miseries
That have wilted and faded into nothingness.
What glorious and tumultuous floods of expectations,
What arresting Everests of glittering hopes
Have dwindled and shrivelled into the common place!

Nevertheless why mourn and grieve the transformation?
Rather let our hearts melt and overflow
With ripe and mellow thankfulness
That we once had such supreme confidence.
For had we started devoid of soaring hopes,
With fettered and wingless expectations,

To what dank depths would we have sunk at 49?
So let us rejoice at our miniscule and unrecognised achievements.
For, who ever realised the wholeness of his dreams?
Who was it who so aptly said
Better to have loved and lost
Than never to have loved at all?

May 1978

Magic

There is magic in a dying fire!
A magic that gently steals away
Consciousness of the world around
And leaves me in a world of my own;
In a dreamland as full of peace and beauty
As a cloudless sunset on a quiet evening.

There is magic in a dying fire!
The little blue flames that playfully
Hug the remnant pieces of wood
As if to tickle them into flame,
The ripe-red of the serene embers
In an unmatched beauty parade
Changing into other indescribable reds
Sparkling bright as a setting sun,
And then into a rich pale grey ash
Now and then an elfin crack
As embers break off the wood.
    Absolute pure magic!

December 1952

The things I miss

To lie on my back on the warm green grass,
And silently watch clouds racing in the sky,
To see in their changing shapes, stalking lions,
Faces of aged men, and soft heaps of cotton.

To watch the man in the moon
With his bundle of firewood,
To feel and believe the moon and him
Following me wherever I go
Around the house and into the *lusuku,*
To be sure the man in the moon
Peeps through the silvery banana leaves
And laughs at me hiding from him!

    These things I miss.

The smell of earth after a shower
At the end of the long hot drought,
The smoke of the cow dung fire in the evening,
The breath of cows munching cud in the kraal;
Rain on banana leaves and on the thatch;
To be sure I needn't get up while it rains
To pull the blanket up to my neck
And feel the warmth of the bed against
The cold and the wet outside.

    All these I miss.

To be able once more
To listen to the song of birds
And invent words to fit them,
Or to be petrified in the silence of night
By sounds all too clear and common now.
The howling of dogs in the mating season,

The hoot of the owl or the deeper hoot
Of the Gold-Crested Crane;
To lie breathless and numb with fear
Believing it was a wizard playing,
Whilst all the time an Ankole artist
Plays his flute in the silence of night;
All these were mine once
But alas they no longer belong.
How I wish I could retrieve them.

lusuku: a plantain or banana garden

The insolent slave

Leave me alone!
Why must you bother me all the time
Commanding my unwilling attention
Through your unceasing prattle and chatter?
You are a slave, and I, your master.

I shall issue the commands,
Not you; insolent wretch!
And, STOP FUSSING ABOUT ME
As if I was a six-year old!
"It is time to do this,
It is time to do that"
"You cannot afford to stay
One little minute longer"
"You've woken up too late"
        My God!

You even are impertinent enough
To tell me when I should feel hungry!
For heaven's sake SHUT UP!!
You insolent watch!

Fits of depression

Out of the immensity of void
With the deadly silent speed
Of guided missiles in space
These spiked, dipped-in-poison arrows
Converge unerringly onto me.
They tear the mind deeply and cruelly
Leaving me sprawled in the mud of agony
Writhing, coiling and uncoiling
Like a beheaded snake slowly dying.

Their vile poison painfully and swiftly
Spreads through my writhing hulk
Like a drop of black ink dropped
Into a glass of transparent water
Forming exotic fancy patterns
Of beautiful ephemeral curves
Till all is one dark mess of confusion.
For a while I lie numb and bewildered
Stuck in the confusion muds of feeling.

Slowly and fitfully, like a bubble
Pushed by succeeding bubbles
Finally escapes the length of a drinking straw,
Reason emerges from the morass
Of bleeding primeval feelings
Dispels the dark suffocating clouds,
Dissolves the sickening coating of hurt feelings
Polishes faith, confidence and reason
Till my true mettle sparkles again

    And I live.

I refuse to take your brotherly hand

Your nails are black with dirt brother,
And your palms are clammy with sweat.
I refuse to take the hand you extend in help.
I shall not join hands with you brother
For unclean hands make me uneasy
For filthy fingernails rob me of my pride.

You argue, gesticulating with your once
Impeccably clean and beautiful hands,
That before long it shall not matter
For everybody is delving and digging
And all shall have hands dripping with dirt;

That nobody shall know what clean hands look like
And there shall be comfort in the dirty crowd
And enough to eat, for there are good yields
When the stinking manure is well dug in
With strong and bold hands in time.

Are you going blind brother?
I ask how many, have the sludge
Or the strong and bold hands like yours
With which to dig and delve?
Brother the hands of many are too weak with hunger
And for many the sludge is out of reach
And yet for others the stink is too nauseating!
But all have eyes and hunger fills them with anger
As they watch your fingernails fill with dirt!

I have seen hungry envious eyes
Watching silently through your chain-link fence.
I have seen eyes in deep sunken sockets
Burning with anger intently watching you.

I have seen parched mouths water with saliva
And heard the rumbling of hollow empty stomachs
As they watched you feed the dog with meat
From the heavy yields of the city sludge.

Have you entirely forgotten brother
The fragrance and comfort of clean hands?
The confidence the peace you have when you know
You'll leave no ugly smudge upon the street?
Don't you shake hands with fat dirty men
With the dirty clammy palms?

Let me alone brother and from the top of the cliff
Don't offer me your dirty hand in help.
Let me trudge the long way up
For the short cuts are soiled and slippery
Your palms are clammy with the sweat of fear
And your fingernails are clogged with dirt.

Mosquito and I

Go 'way!
Joe said,
Waving his hand
As if brushing away
A pernicious mosquito.

She stretched a beggar's hand
And said, Babi sah.
Babi, most unconcerned,
Continued sucking his thumb
Upon Mosquito's shoulder.
Babi sah!
GO 'WAY, Joe hissed;
And Akiiki said,
In a language foreign to her,
This woman is fake.
Babi is fat and contented
But she keeps on saying
Babi sah, Babi sah!

Babi looked alright
But Mosquito was thin and starving
I felt for a rupee in my pocket.

Mosquito noticed my search
Babi sah!
With her hand outstretched.
Unkempt black sisal-hair
Like Fay's favourite doll.
Wide white desperate eyes
Which seemed to say to me
You are very kind sah!
Long, bone-and-skin arms

Filthy nails on tapering fingers,
Bare feet sprinkled with fine dust.

I clutch the rupee
And I am calculating
Whether it should be two or three;
She reminds me so much
Of Fay's miserable doll.

Joe notices my weak intentions
Aa-aa-he says,
Gently pushes me on
And in a language foreign to her
If you do that, the rest will
Close onto us and buzz
Around us like *obubu*
On a bunch of over-ripe bananas.
Babi sah, she pleads.
I irresolutely clutch
And unclutch the coins.
But Joe this time grabs my shoulder
And pushes me firmly away
While he barks, GO 'WAY.

We pile into the Benz 280
And the turbaned Singh
Notices Mosquito following,
Starts the power-packed engine
Barks severely at Mosquito
In a language foreign to me
Waves a threatening finger at her.

Turbaned Singh says
With a face contorted
With put-on disgust

Babi sah, Babi sah! He repeats
And spits a huge red spittle
On the racing black tarmac
As we zoom away.

As for me,
I kept seeing that thin
Outstretched hand of Mosquito,
While 'Babi sah' deafened my ears
And the rupees cut into my hand.

obubu: fruit fly (drosophila)

May 1971

Women - my bane

It was raining softly and soothingly
I was cosy and smiling in my dreams
    Then mother came!
Rudely pulled off my blanket,
Get up you lazy boy, she shouted.
Other children are half-way to the school!
Get up and dress immediately.
But mother it is raining, I objected pleadingly.
Shut up and dress up you stupid boy;
And she stormed away.

I quickly retrieved my blanket
Curled myself back into it.
Soon I was in class, and had repeated
All my multiplication tables correctly.
Teacher had not cut my fingers
With that horrible ruler of his.
I was jubilant! Then mother came!
Sprinkled freezing water on my face.
I jumped out of bed fully awake!
And ran all the way to school.

I am sixty and retired.
It is Saturday and raining besides!
I am rudely shaken out of my dreams
I blink unseeingly but lo and behold!
It is my wife with a steaming cup of coffee.
You're late you lazy old man!
What the hell are you waking me up for?
I shout at her. Can't I enjoy my retirement?
You asked me to, and you know why,
She retorts and walks away.
I jump out of bed fully awake.
Don't even taste my coffee
Indeed I am late!
Oh God! Women my bane!

Muyenga, February 1990

The tenth commandment
I have seen others
Limp around awkwardly -
Heard many vent their feelings
Vehemently and intelligibly.
My heart swells to bursting point
With envy, jealousy and pain!

But the men of God
From high and exalted pulpits
Pontificate with infallible authority
Thou shalt not be jealous
Of your neighbour's wife
Not even of his lowly donkey!

I listen with a secret smile
More sad than bemused.
I reluctantly forgive them
Their profoundly dogmatic sermons
For how could they possibly know
The pure innocence and depth
Of my envy and jealousy.

Harare, 4 February, 1989

Not forever courageously

I have not revelled in green pastures
Basking contentedly in the warm sun,
By the clear swift flowing streams.
Instead I have wearily trudged the long
Dangerously steep and rugged pathway;
Not with ease, but always courageously
Often with tears streaming down my cheeks!

One question keeps tormenting me
Why should I forever trudge this
Rugged, steep and dangerous path?
I desperately long to also enjoy
The lush green pastures and
To bask by, and quench my thirst
From the bubbling and clear sweet waters.

Courage is not inexhaustible and
Anguish can maim and even kill.

1996

The simmering amalgam

I am a simmering amalgam
I am a blend, an alloy.
I am a simmering motley amalgam
Changing texture and potency,
Size, density, weight, and hues
With the unstable intensity of life!

My mind boils and simmers,
Bears the rending stresses and strains,
The painful expansions and contractions
Of a thousand varied and unequal minds
Being compounded, smelted and fused
To form a wholesome entity.

My mind shudders and shivers
Battling ever unceasingly
With a hundred thousand thoughts
Each single day that passes by.
Never resting a moment from
Sampling, weighing, and measuring
Sorting, discarding, and storing
Striving to achieve some order
In the milling chaotic thoughts.

With joy flashing briefly in and out
While sorrow lumbers painfully on
With love and hate, anger and laughter
My senses vibrate and tremble
Like the innocent strings
Of a well-tuned harp plucked
Discordantly by a mischievous imp.

My actions are of mixed origin
Strong-limbed courage
Is a child of trembling fear,
What often appears cowardly
Is born of courageous decisions.
Charity selfishly craves recognition;
While Humility is pregnant with Pride.

Oh! mixtures abound with life!
They smoulder, choking in smoke,
Burst into brilliant and beautiful flame,
Are burnt out and turned to ash.
They freeze, thaw, grow warm again
Blossom, seed, wither, and die.
Purity is always dead and cold!

I am a simmering stress-torn amalgam;
A concoction of many and varied blends;
A live strong alloy in the melting pot!

PART VII

OF LOVE AND ALL THAT

Our love

Our love was a dream
That starts in joyous bliss
And ends in a nightmare
Heart-rending and soul-freezing!

It was a beautiful dawn
Proclaiming a wonderful day
But was overrun and eclipsed
By destructive violent storms.

It was a moon in the fairest sky
Radiating enchantment unrivalled
Suddenly swallowed by darkest clouds
Driven by jealous winds from nowhere.

The joys, we shared;
The anguish was mine -
    Alone!

The reunion

As the waters of a stream
Divided by an island
Meet at the other side
And with renewed vigour flow
Our love deeper and stronger flows!

As all the countryside
Looks, cleaner, after the rains
Have washed the dusty skies
As clean is our love now!

As fresh as a strong wind
Before dawn adorns the sky
With streaks of untainted colours
Is our love now!

As the water glitters on the lake
When the moon suddenly
Moves out of an enveloping cloud
Thus glitters our love now!

24 July 1952

To the persistent ghost

One day you will haunt me no more.
One day you will torture me no more
And all the charms you hold for me
By fairer and truer charms will replaced be.
Thy image shall fade into nothingness
And bright reality shall eclipse you
As does fair dawn the night.
Your charms shall forgotten be
And the sting in my heart
Be usurped by a thrill!

April 1954

Assault

I shall sue you for assault!
For your eyes and your lips
Conspire in a wonder smile
Which spreads all over your face
Sending deadly arrows into my heart
And I stand speechless
Stunned and breathless!

Yet, I shall be protected I demand it.
There is a law against assault.
I shall surely sue you.
Ah! but what an empty hope!
What judge can ever utter
Sentence against such a witch?
He too will be surely assaulted!

You have only to stand in the dock
And smile with those eyes and lips
And the bewigged learned judge
And all his motly simple jury
Shall immediately bewitched be!
They will stare speechless.
Stunned and breathless!

So, sorcerer, I shall not sue
I shall instead assault you -
Viciously and ruthlessly.
I shall blind those bewitching eyes
And arrest your vivacious lips
With long searching kisses.
Thus my already bruised heart

Shall delightfully be avenged
Though I may, in the sweet battle,
Lose my head!

Love for Margaret

Our love was as abrupt and brief
As the beautiful coffee blossom;
A fragrant, stunning, white purity
Which bursts onto the world overnight
Dazzles and intoxicates for a day
And is gone!

Moments that live forever

We sat in the back seat
Of the now mended and speeding car.
In front the bright headlights
Tore the gathering darkness
Creating a cosy twilight at the back.
It had been a wearisome day
But now we sighed with relief!
     We kissed,
And to this day I swear I saw,
In that cosy darkness,
Your eyes glow with a gentle light
Like two glow worms at dusk!
I saw your beautiful smile
In the glow worm light from your eyes.
     again I swear
Your eyes were two bright glow-worms
- Or were they just a reflection of mine?

I dare not pull you apart

Do not ask me why I love you;
For if I were to pull you apart
And analyse you minutely
Like clever critics do a poem;
If I were to sit and ponder
Whether it is the mysterious glow
In your eyes when you smile
Or the ripeness of your lips;
Were I to dissect the rhythm
Or the freshness of your ideas:
Were I to say it is the often illogical
Liveliness and intensity of
Your argument when excited,
I could not put you together again
And I love you as I surely do.
I am not a learned critic
I do not love fragmented
And disjointed parts of you.
I love the sum total
Of your personality
I dare not pull you apart!!

www.ingramcontent.com/pod-product-compliance
Lightning Source LLC
Chambersburg PA
CBHW071215160426
43196CB00012B/2309